D1537920

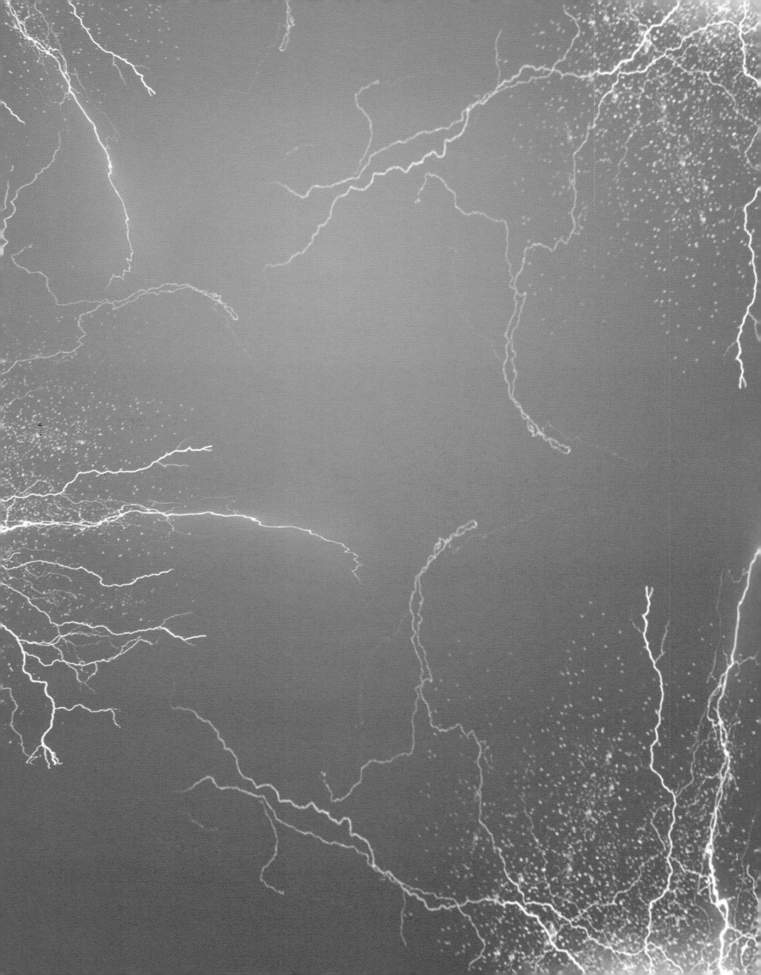

# SPARKS, SHOCKS, AND SECRETS

Explore electricity and use science to survive

Richard and Louise Spilsbury

Smart Apple Media

Published by Smart Apple Media, an imprint of Black Rabbit Books
P.O. Box 3263, Mankato, Minnesota 56002
www.smartapplemedia.com

Published by arrangement with Watts Publishing, London.

Cataloging-in-Publication Data is available from the Library of Congress
ISBN:  978-1-62588-148-9   (library binding)
ISBN:  978-1-62588-400-8   (paperback)
ISBN:  978-1-62588-583-8   (eBook)

Printed in the United States by CG Book Printers
North Mankato, Minnesota

PO 1723
3-2015

Picture Credits
Shutterstock: Aninka, Anthony Berenyi, Artazum, Astragal, Boris Rabtsevich, Brykaylo Yuriy, Christos Georghiou, D.Bond, David Hughes, dramaj, FreshStudio, geographlo, Goldution, Graeme Dawes, Gwoeii, Horiyan, ilolab, Jenn HulsKasia Bialasiewicz, Kuznetsov Alexey, Meewezen Photography, Megin, MichaelJayBerlin, MustafaNC, naihei, Natykach Nataliia, Nikolai Pozdeev, pics721, romawka, Sfocato, Slobodan Djajic, Sooa, Sue Smith, Taweesak Jarearnsin, Tristan tan, Tungphoto, Vladm, Wuttichok Painichiwarapun, Zastolskiy Victor.

**Bold** words in the text are included in the glossary

# WHO'S WHO?

## JESS

Jess is a bit of a daredevil. She's always first to try something new. She loves skateboarding, climbing, and adventure stories.

## BEN

Ben is a bit of a gadget fanatic. He carries his backpack with him at all times and it's full of useful—and not so useful—stuff.

## AMELIE

Amelie is a science whiz. She's not a know-it-all, but she often has the right answers. She doesn't like getting her clothes dirty and her hair messed up.

## ZAC

Zac is the youngest and although he never wants to be left out, he can get a bit nervous and is easily spooked.

# CONTENTS

# SPARKS!

"An **electronics kit**!" shouts Amelie happily. "That's exactly what I wanted!"

"We know. It's all you've talked about for weeks," groans Zac.

"Before you play with it and forget we're even here, can we please have some birthday cake?" asks Jess.

"Um... my mom's stepped out, but I think it's down in the kitchen," answers Amelie.

Suddenly, there is a huge spark and all the lights go out.

"Aaarrggh!" screams Zac. "What happened?"

"Maybe a robber cut a wire and broke the electricity **circuit** in the house. He needs darkness so he can creep in unnoticed..." teases Ben.

"Stop it, Ben. That's not possible," says Jess.

"Yes it is," says Amelie. "Ben, give me your flashlight and I'll show you."

**WHAT DO YOU THINK?**

Is Amelie right? Could the lights have all gone out because a circuit was broken?

# PROVE IT!

Investigate circuits yourself.
You need:

- electrical wire
- electrical tape
- small **bulb** (from a flashlight)
- elastic band
- 1.5v battery

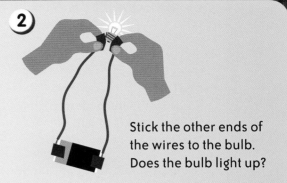

Stick the other ends of the wires to the bulb. Does the bulb light up?

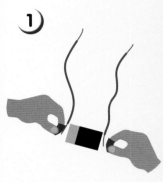

Ask an adult to help you cut two lengths of wire, each about 8 inches (20 cm) long, and then carefully cut about 1¼ inches (3 cm) of the plastic coating off the ends of those wires. Use the tape to attach one end of each wire to opposite ends of the battery.

Remove one of the wires from the bulb or the battery so the circuit is broken. What happens now?

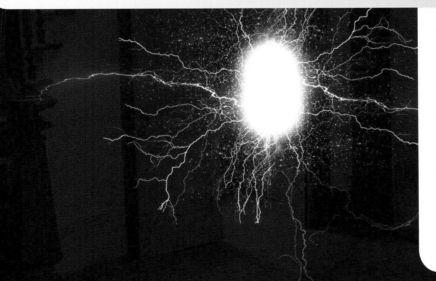

## WHY IT WORKS

Amelie is right. Electricity flows from a power **source** (the battery) around a circuit. It passes through the wire and other parts, such as bulbs, and returns to the power source. If there is a gap in the circuit, no electricity will flow. The wires in a house run in circuits that include all the lightbulbs in every room.

# POWERING UP

"No-ooo!" cries Zac. "Ben, your stupid flashlight only lasted a few minutes. Put a new battery in it, quick!"

"Bad news. There are no more batteries in my backpack," sighs Ben.

"There's enough moonlight for me to see a little bit. Check out my new trick!" says Jess, juggling with four lemons.

"There's no time for that," says Zac. "It's creepy in here. Please find a light."

"My new kit shows me how to use lemons as batteries," says Amelie. "C'mon, Jess. Hand them over."

"No way—that's just crazy!" snorts Jess.

Amelie shoots an annoyed look at Jess. "Fine, I'll use my kit to show you."

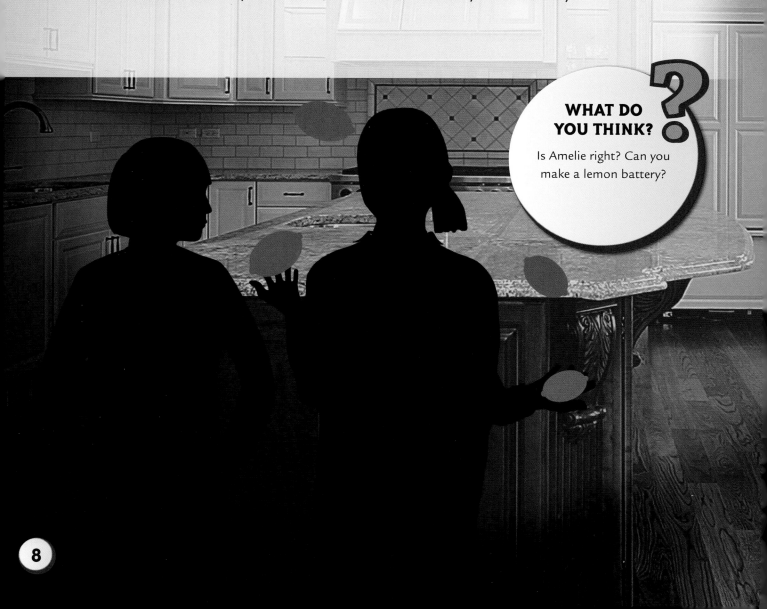

## WHAT DO YOU THINK?

Is Amelie right? Can you make a lemon battery?

Investigate whether a lemon can make electricity.
You need:

- copper electrical wire ● wire clippers ● lemon
- steel paper clip ● sheet of coarse sandpaper

**①**

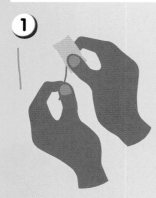

Ask an adult to help you. Straighten the paper clip and use the wire clippers to cut 1½ inches (4 cm) off it. Trim 1½ inches (4 cm) of plastic coating off the copper wire, and cut off that bare wire. Use sandpaper to smooth any rough edges off both wires.

**②**

Squeeze the lemon gently or roll it on a table to make it juicier. Push the two wire pieces into the lemon, close together, but not touching.

**③**

Touch the tip of your wet tongue to the free ends of the two wires. The tip of your tongue should tingle!

## WHY IT WORKS

In a lemon battery, as in a real battery, **chemical energy** changes into electrical energy. The juice in the lemon **reacts** differently with the steel wire than the copper wire and this makes a tiny electric **current** flow through your tongue.

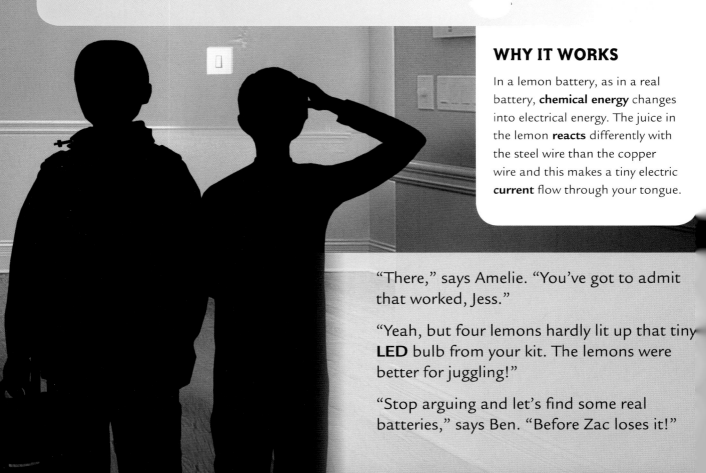

"There," says Amelie. "You've got to admit that worked, Jess."

"Yeah, but four lemons hardly lit up that tiny **LED** bulb from your kit. The lemons were better for juggling!"

"Stop arguing and let's find some real batteries," says Ben. "Before Zac loses it!"

# WHO'S WATCHING US?

"'Look! There's something out there," shouts Zac suddenly. "And it's watching us."

"Wow, I think he's right this time," says Jess. "I can see eyes glaring at us from the dark."

"It's probably just a cat or a fox," says Amelie. "Don't panic. Ben's found batteries in a drawer, and he'll turn his flashlight on soon."

"I won't—it's not working," sighs Ben.

"The batteries are probably in the wrong way," says Jess.

"What difference would that make?" cry Zac and Amelie together.

## WHAT DO YOU THINK?

Is Jess right? Do batteries only work if they are the right way around?

Investigate how batteries work.
You need:

- flashlight that uses two batteries (with no batteries in it)
- two batteries (that fit the flashlight)
- piece of 8 inch-long (20 cm) electrical wire (with 1¼ inch {3 cm} of plastic coating taken off the ends)
- electrical tape

**2** Tape two batteries together with the positive (+) end of one battery touching the positive (+) end of the other. Stand the flat end on the free end of the wire. Press the metal tip at the bottom of the flashlight bulb against the end of the top battery. What happens?

**1** Unscrew the top of the flashlight to take off the part that holds the bulb. Wrap one end of the wire around the bottom of the bulb holder and tape it on.

**3** Repeat step 2, but with the positive (+) end of one battery touching the negative (-) end of the other. What happens?

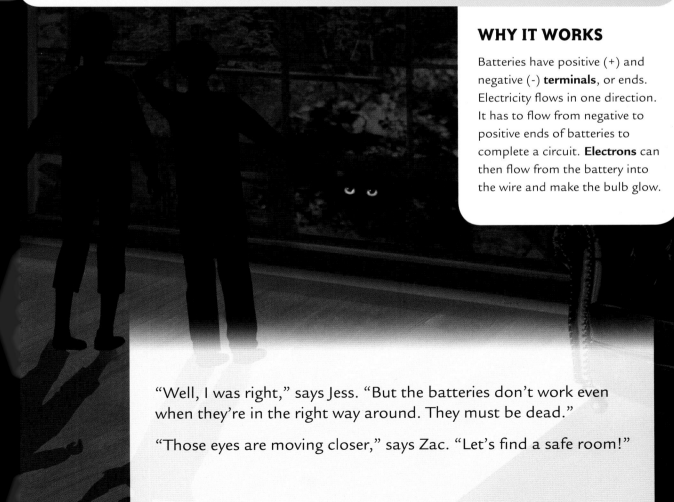

## WHY IT WORKS

Batteries have positive (+) and negative (-) **terminals**, or ends. Electricity flows in one direction. It has to flow from negative to positive ends of batteries to complete a circuit. **Electrons** can then flow from the battery into the wire and make the bulb glow.

"Well, I was right," says Jess. "But the batteries don't work even when they're in the right way around. They must be dead."

"Those eyes are moving closer," says Zac. "Let's find a safe room!"

# A SPOOKY ENCOUNTER

"Wh... wh... what's that?" trembles Jess, pointing to a tall white figure that looms threateningly over them as they stumble into the next room.

"It loo... loo... looks like a ghost to me!" yells Zac.

"Run!" shouts Ben.

"Wait!" shouts Amelie sharply. "It's not a ghost. It's just some sheets hanging over ladders and stuff because Mom and Dad are decorating in here. There's nothing to be scared of."

"Phew!" sigh the other three.

"I'll use two bulbs from my kit to make us a light," Amelie continues. "But I need another battery—the light won't be bright enough with just the one battery I've found. Stop messing around and help me look, will you?"

"We can carry the light around on a tray to help us see where we're going," adds Ben. "I'll try and find a tray while you three look for batteries."

**WHAT DO YOU THINK?**

Is Amelie right? Do you need more batteries to make bulbs brighter?

Investigate bulbs and batteries.
You need:

- two long and two shorter pieces of electrical wire (with 1¼ inches {3 cm} of plastic coating off all the ends)
- electrical tape ● two 1.5v batteries
- two small 1.5v bulbs

Set up a circuit like you did in the experiment on page 7, with the two long wires, one bulb and one battery.

Now remove the end of one wire from the battery and attach it to another bulb. Then use a short piece of wire between the two bulbs to complete the circuit. What happens?

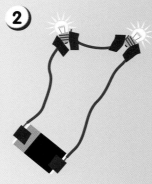

Now remove the end of one wire from the battery and attach it to another battery. If you have removed the wire from the positive (+) end of the first battery, then you must attach it to the positive (+) end of the second battery. Use a short piece of wire between the two batteries to complete the circuit. What happens?

## WHY IT WORKS

When you add another bulb, both bulbs get dimmer (less bright). Each bulb uses some of the electrical energy so there is less for each bulb. Both bulbs get brighter when another battery is added to the circuit. There are more **volts** to push more electric current through the circuit, so the current flows faster and can work harder to light up both bulbs. Amelie is right.

# BUZZING BADDIES

"Now we've made a light, can we please get some cake?" begs Jess, heading to the kitchen. "Being scared makes me hungry."

"Well, you'll be starving in a minute—listen!" cries Zac. "It sounds like giant, jagged claws are scratching the front door. Something is trying to get in..."

"It's just a branch scraping across the wall outside, Zac. Calm down or you'll freak us all out!" snaps Amelie.

"How about making an alarm with that kit of yours, Amelie?" says Ben. "Make a pressure **switch** so when someone steps on the doormat a buzzer goes off to warn us they're coming."

# PROVE IT!

Investigate making a pressure switch to sound a buzzer. You need:

- 1.5v battery ● scissors
- three pieces of wire (with 1¼ inches {3 cm} of plastic covering stripped from each end)
- buzzer ● aluminium foil ● plastic bottle
- paper fasteners ● cardboard ● electrical tape

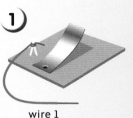

**1** Ask an adult to help you cut a strip of curved plastic from the bottle and cover it with foil. Then ask this adult to use one blade of the scissors to pierce a hole at one end of the strip. This is your switch. Wrap a piece of wire (wire 1) around a paper fastener. Attach the switch to the cardboard by putting the wire-wrapped fastener through the hole in the switch and then through the cardboard.

wire 1

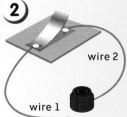

**2** Connect one end of another wire (wire 2) to a paper fastener that goes through the cardboard under where the switch lands when you press it down. Connect the other end of the wire to a buzzer.

wire 2

wire 1

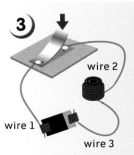

**3** Attach the free end of wire 1 to the battery. Attach a third wire (wire 3) between the buzzer and the other end of the battery. What happens when you push down on the switch?

wire 2

wire 1

wire 3

## WHAT DO YOU THINK?

Is Ben right? Can you make a pressure switch to activate a buzzer?

## WHY IT WORKS

When you press the switch, the circuit is complete and the buzzer works. When the switch isn't pressed down, the circuit is incomplete and the buzzer doesn't work. Ben is right, you can make a burglar alarm from a buzzer and a switch that closes a circuit when pressed.

# INTRUDERS IN THE DARK

"Guys, I think we're too late to make an alarm for the back door. Look!" whispers Jess. Her hand shakes as she points towards what look like two figures lurking in the shadows outside.

"I knew it! I told you intruders were trying to get in," hisses Zac.

"Relax," sighs Ben, after a few moments of tense silence. "Those 'intruders' are clothes on the washing line outside! The breeze is making them move, that's all."

"Phew!" sighs Amelie. "Now help me find some other material to make another alarm circuit. I've run out of wire."

"I've got string in my backpack," offers Ben. "Will that do?"

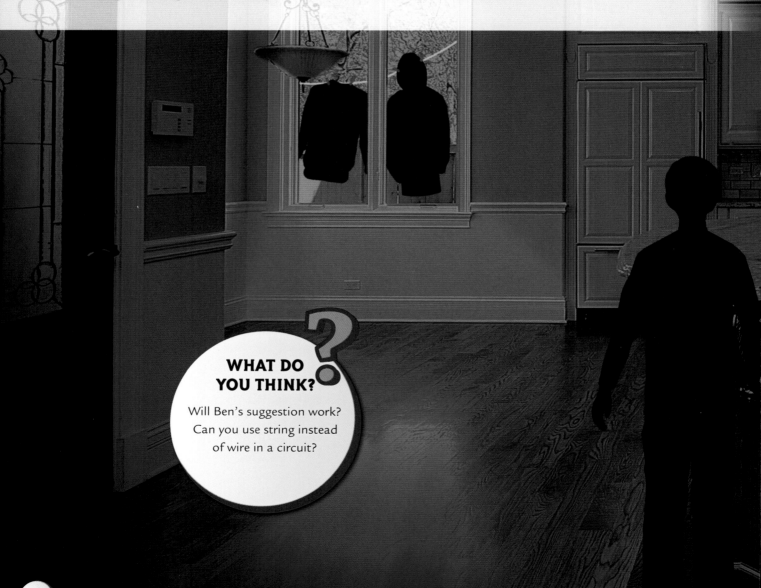

**WHAT DO YOU THINK?**

Will Ben's suggestion work? Can you use string instead of wire in a circuit?

# PROVE IT!

Investigate which materials make good conductors of electricity.
You need:

- six different materials, such as: string, a metal spoon, a plastic spoon, aluminium foil, an eraser, a pencil (with both ends sharpened)
- three pieces of wire (with 1¼ inches {3 cm} of plastic covering stripped from each end)
- 1.5v battery ● light bulb

 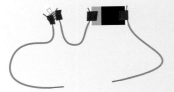

Make a simple circuit. Attach one wire between the negative (-) terminal of the battery and a bulb. Attach one end of the second wire to the positive (+) end of the battery. Attach one end of the third wire to the bulb. Leave a gap between these last two wires.

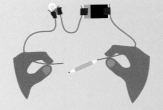

Place one of your test materials between the open ends of the last two wires. Touch both wires to opposite ends of the material. Repeat with the other test materials. Record what happens each time.

## WHY IT WORKS

A **conductor** is a material that allows electricity to flow through it easily. Metals are conductors. Some materials do not conduct electricity. These are called **insulators**. Non-metals, such as string, are insulators rather than conductors. Ben is wrong about being able to use string to make a circuit.

# NOISES IN THE ATTIC

"What's that noise now?" hisses Zac. "Amelie, why did you bring us up here? I can't take much more of this!"

"It sounds like footsteps in the attic," whispers Jess. "It's creeping me out, too."

"Ben and I will go and look," says Amelie. "But we'll have to take the light. I'll draw you a **circuit diagram** so you can use my kit to make another circuit."

"What's a circuit diagram?" demands Jess. "And how is it going to help us?"

"It isn't going to help at all right now," says Ben gently. "Amelie, we haven't got any extra batteries, or another light so they can read the circuit diagram!"

Amelie looks embarrassed. "Sorry, I'm so nervous that I'm not thinking straight! Circuit diagrams are very useful—just not in our particular situation. I'm afraid you guys will have to wait in the dark for now."

## WHAT DO YOU THINK?

What does Amelie mean? How can a circuit diagram help people build circuits?

# PROVE IT!

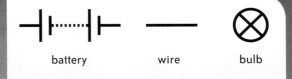

| | | |
|---|---|---|
| battery | wire | bulb |
| buzzer | switch (off) | switch (on) |

**1** Look at the **circuit symbols** above, and try to learn them so you can use them from memory.

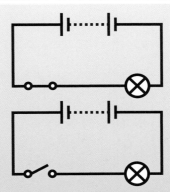

**2** If you made both of these circuits, which one do you think would work?

## WHY IT WORKS

The top circuit diagram is the one that would work because it shows the switch in the 'on' position. This means that the switch is closed and the circuit is complete, so electricity can flow continuously around it. Circuit diagrams don't show exactly where things are in a circuit in real life, just how the **components** connect together. We use them because describing complex circuits in words or making accurate life-like drawings of them is difficult and can take a long time.

# SHOCKS!

"Zac, I promise you there was nothing in the attic," says Ben patiently. "That noise must have just been an old window banging in the wind."

"Well, if you say so..." Zac says, sounding unconvinced.

"You can check yourself if you don't believe it," snaps Jess. "I want to stay down here in the kitchen so that I can finally get some cake, but you're welcome to go up alone."

Zac scowls and stays where he is.

"We've got to find the cake first," says Amelie, peering into a small, dark cupboard.

"Let me try the lights again," says Ben, shaking the water off his hands after washing the attic dust from them at the sink.

"Nooo!" shouts Jess, leaping forwards. "Don't touch the light switch with wet hands. You'll get an **electric shock**!"

## WHAT DO YOU THINK?

Is Jess right to be worried? Can water give us an electric shock?

## PROVE IT!

Investigate whether water can conduct electricity.
You need:

- three pieces of wire (with 1¼ inches {3 cm} of plastic covering stripped from each end) • 1.5v battery • bulb • plastic cup
- water • salt • teaspoon

Make a simple circuit. Attach one wire between the negative (-) terminal of the battery and a bulb. Attach one end of the second wire to the positive (+) end of the battery. Attach one end of the third wire to the bulb. Leave a gap between these last two wires.

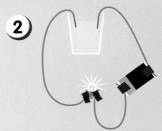

Put some water into the cup and stir two teaspoons of salt into it. Dangle the two free ends of the wires into the water. What happens?

### WHY IT WORKS

The bulb should light up because water, particularly salty water, conducts electricity. Human bodies are two-thirds water, with salts **dissolved** in that water. So if water passes an electric current into your fingers, the current can spread through your body. This gives you an electric shock, which can be very dangerous. Jess is right, you must never touch electrical switches with wet hands.

# KEEPING SECRETS

"Shh... I can definitely hear something. Maybe someone is trying to get in the house after all," says Amelie, looking worried. "I didn't say anything before in case it scared you, but my dad's latest **invention** is upstairs. Maybe another company wants to steal it?"

"I knew it, I knew it!" says Zac, triumphantly.

"Well, we need to hide it somewhere safe before they get in," says Jess.

"Yeah, and make a secret code to say where it is in case we get kidnapped!" suggests Ben.

"Okay, let's use my new kit," says Amelie excitedly. "We'll make a circuit quiz board. The first letter of each answer put together can spell the hiding place. Dad will get that."

"Genius!" says Ben admiringly.

**WHAT DO YOU THINK?**

Can you use electric circuit boards to hide answers?

Make your own electric circuit quiz board.
You need:

- thin sheet of tagboard
- 12 paper fasteners
- six pieces of 4 inch-long (10 cm) electrical wire
  with bare ends
- 1.5v battery  ● 1.5–2.5v bulb

## WHY IT WORKS

The bulb should light up each time you touch the fasteners beside a matching question and answer. This is because the continuous wire between the correct question and answer pair completes a circuit.

**1)** 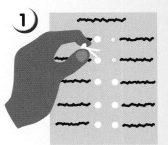 On the front of the tagboard, down the left-hand side, write a set of questions. Then write the answers down the right-hand side, but make sure they are listed in a different order to the questions. Draw a dot beside each question and answer. Push a paper fastener through the tagboard at each dot.

**2)**  Turn the tagboard over and use wires to connect each question with the correct answer. Use the paper fasteners to hold the wires in place, making sure that their arms don't touch each other. Keep turning the tagboard over to check you are getting this right.

**3)** 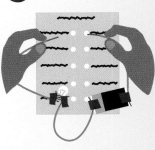 Set up a simple circuit with a battery and a bulb (see page 21), leaving one wire from the battery and one wire from the bulb unattached. Ask a friend to touch the wires to the fasteners beside one question and the answer they think is right. If the bulb lights up, they are correct!

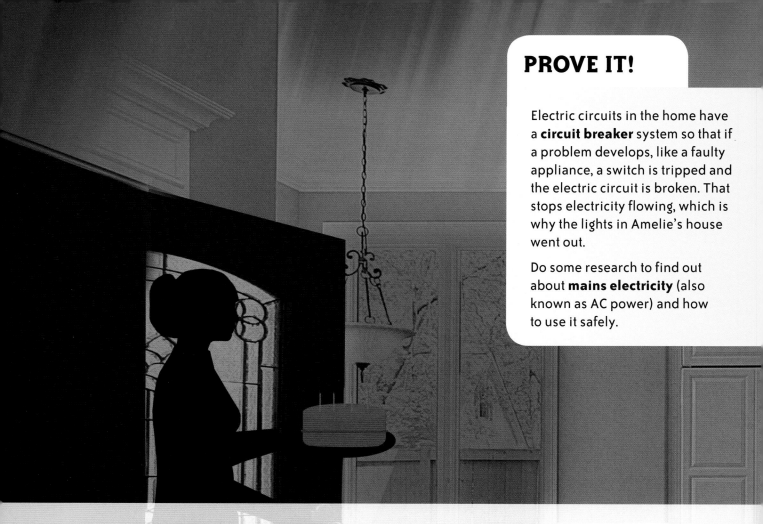

## PROVE IT!

Electric circuits in the home have a **circuit breaker** system so that if a problem develops, like a faulty appliance, a switch is tripped and the electric circuit is broken. That stops electricity flowing, which is why the lights in Amelie's house went out.

Do some research to find out about **mains electricity** (also known as AC power) and how to use it safely.

# SAFE AT LAST?

"I can hear footsteps right outside! Come on, let's hide—quick!" whispers Zac.

"I hear them, too, and they're getting closer," warns Ben.

The friends watch in horror as the handle turns and the back door creaks slowly open...

"Surprise!" shouts a cheerful, familiar voice.

"Mom!" yells Amelie with relief. "We thought a burglar cut off the electricity and was trying to get in to steal Dad's secret invention!"

"What?! No, don't worry, Dad's new invention is safe at his lab at work. The only secret here is this birthday cake I've been out to buy," replies Mom. "The lights probably went out because a **trip switch** was triggered. I'll fix it in a moment."

"Hooray!" shouts Jess. "What a night. We definitely deserve a BIG slice of birthday cake!

**1**

Find out more about how mains electricity is generated (made) at power stations and how it travels hundreds of miles from power stations to our homes. Why shouldn't you fly a kite near electricity pylons and overhead power lines?

**2**

When cables bring electricity to our homes, it travels through wires in walls and we use it from light switches and plugs in the walls. Find out why you shouldn't overload sockets and why you must never put anything other than a plug in a socket.

**3**

Make a poster to tell people about staying safe with electricity, using the information you've found in your research.

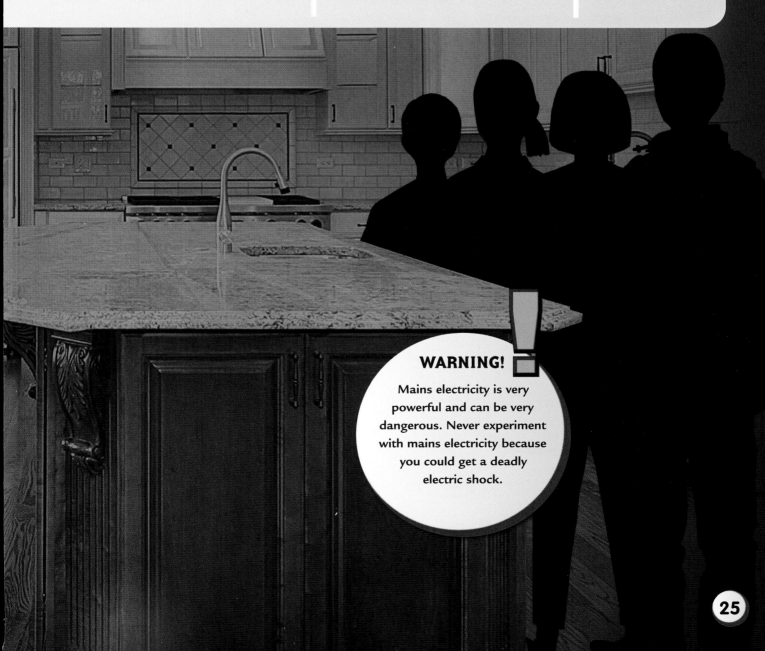

### WARNING!

Mains electricity is very powerful and can be very dangerous. Never experiment with mains electricity because you could get a deadly electric shock.

# QUIZ

**1** **What is an electric circuit?**

a) a wire

b) a path or loop along which electricity can travel

c) somewhere people race battery-powered cars

**2** **Why is a lemon battery like a real battery?**

a) they are both yellow

b) they both contain electricity

c) they both contain chemical energy that can change into electrical energy

**3** **How should you connect two batteries to make a complete circuit?**

a) connect the positive end of one to the positive end of the other

b) connect the negative end of one to the negative end of the other

c) connect the negative end of one to the positive end of the other

**4** **What happens if you add a bulb to a circuit that has one battery and one bulb?**

a) both bulbs go off

b) both bulbs get brighter

c) both bulbs get dimmer

**5** **What happens if you add a battery to a circuit that has one battery and two bulbs?**

a) both bulbs get brighter

b) both bulbs get dimmer

c) one bulb gets brighter than the other

remember! | 9 b | 10 c | 11 b | 12 a   How did you do?

8 c - well, to be fair 'a' is true too, but we're talking about electrical conductors here,

**6** In a simple circuit, why does a bulb light when you close the switch?

a) because the switch produces electricity

b) because closing the switch completes the circuit

c) because closing the switch breaks the circuit

**7** Will the bulbs in this circuit light up?

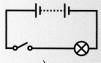

a) yes

b) no

**8** What is a conductor?

a) someone who directs an orchestra

b) a material that doesn't allow electricity to flow through it easily

c) a material that allows electricity to flow through it easily

**9** What do these three circuit diagram symbols show?

a) a bulb, a switch, and a buzzer

b) a battery, a buzzer, and a switch

c) a battery, a buzzer, and a bulb

**11** Why should you never touch an electric switch with wet hands?

a) because a switch won't work when it is wet

b) because electricity can pass easily through water and it could kill you

c) because you'll make it wet for the next person

**10** What should you never do?

a) dance in public

b) clean your teeth on a Tuesday

c) put anything other than a plug into an electrical socket

**12** Electricity from a battery is much weaker than mains electricity. True or false?

a) true

b) false

# FIND OUT MORE

## BOOKS

*Electricity* (Eyewitness)
Dorling Kindersley, 2013

*Electricity* (The Real Scientist Investigates)
Peter Riley, Sea-to-Sea Publications, 2011

*Hands-On Science: Electricity and Magnets*
Kingfisher, 2013

*Investigating Electricity* (How Does Energy Work?)
Sally M. Walker, Lerner Publications, 2011

*Using Electricity* (It's Electric!)
Chris Oxlade, Raintree, 2013

## WEBSITES

Watch this video to find out how to generate your own electricity from vinegar:
https://www.youtube.com/watch?v=Phu--v1WAoU

Get ideas for science fair projects about electricity here:
http://www.education.com/science-fair/electricity-and-magnetism/

Create your own electric model car!
https://www.youtube.com/watch?v=UnxNe_XjlWg

You can find lots of fun electricity experiments here:
http://www.exploratorium.edu/snacks/iconelectricity.html

*Every effort has been made by the publisher to ensure that these websites contain no inappropriate or offensive material. However, because of the nature of the Internet, it is impossible to guarantee that the content of these sites will not be altered. We strongly advise that Internet access is supervised by a responsible adult.*

# GLOSSARY

**bulb**  rounded, glass part of an electric light

**chemical**  to do with chemicals, substances that change upon contact with other things

**circuit**  complete path or loop along which electric current flows

**circuit breaker**  device for stopping the flow of current in an electric circuit

**circuit diagram**  diagram of a circuit that uses simple pictures to represent parts

**circuit symbols**  simple drawing used to represent a part of a circuit, such as a bulb

**component**  part of an electric circuit, such as a battery, wire, or bulb

**conductor**  material that allows electric current to flow through it

**current**  flow of electricity from one place to another

**dissolve**  when a solid seems to disappear into a liquid

**electric shock**  when electricity passes through a person's body and hurts them

**electronics kit**  activity set with equipment for carrying out experiments using electricity

**electrons**  tiny particles in materials that can carry electricity from place to place

**energy**  power to make something work

**insulator**  material that does not allow electric current to flow through it

**invention**  something that a person thinks up and creates

**LED**  stands for "light-emitting diode", a device that gives out light when it comes into contact with electricity

**mains electricity (AC power)**  supply of electricity that people pay to use in their homes and businesses

**react**  when two or more substances come into contact with each other and change to produce one or more new substances

**source**  where something comes from

**switch**  something that makes or breaks a circuit to turn electrical equipment on and off

**terminal**  end point of a battery from or to which electricity can flow

**trip switch**  switch that is triggered in a circuit breaker if an electrical fault develops

**volt**  unit for measuring the force of an electric current

# INDEX